The U. S. Supreme Court

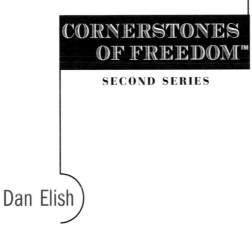

CORNERSTONES OF FREEDOM™

SECOND SERIES

Dan Elish

Children's Press®
An Imprint of Scholastic Inc.
New York • Toronto • London • Auckland • Sydney
Mexico City • New Delhi • Hong Kong
Danbury, Connecticut

Photographs © 2007: AP/Wide World Photos: 37 (Lana Harris), 29, 30, 33, 45; Art Resource, NY: 11, 14 (National Portrait Gallery, Smithsonian Institution), 8 (Réunion des Musées Nationaux); Bridgeman Art Library International Ltd., London/New York/Friedrich Schultz/Hirshhorn Museum, Washington, DC.: 17, 44; Corbis Images: 31 (Bettmann), 3 (Ed Bohon), 40, 41 (Matthew Cavanaugh/epa), 12 (Peter Harholdt), 36 (Wally McNamee), cover top, 39 (Joseph Sohm; ChromoSohm Inc.); Denver Public Library, Western History/Genealogy Department: 21; Folio, Inc.: 24; Getty Images: 38, 45 (Andrew Councill/AFP), 35 (Dirck Halstead/Time Life Pictures), 22 (Hulton Archive), 34 (Brendan Smialowski/AFP), 32 (Diana Walker/Time Life Pictures), cover bottom (Mark Wilson); Library of Congress: 25 (Lewis Wickes Hine), 27 (Frances Benjamin Johnston), 26 (Dorothea Lange), 20 (Napoleon Sarony), 16; National Archives and Records Administration: 6, 7; North Wind Picture Archives: 23; Stock Montage, Inc.: 5, 44; Superstock, Inc./Stock Montage: 13.

Library of Congress Cataloging-in-Publication Data

Elish, Dan.

The U.S. Supreme Court / Dan Elish.

p. cm. — (Cornerstones of freedom. Second series)

Includes bibliographical references and index.

ISBN-13: 978-0-516-23637-7 (lib. bdg.)   978-0-531-20842-7 (pbk.)

ISBN-10: 0-516-23637-7 (lib. bdg.)   0-531-20842-7 (pbk.)

1. United States. Supreme Court—History—Juvenile literature.

2. Constitutional history—United States—Juvenile literature. I. Title.

KF8742.Z9E45 2007

347.73'2609—dc22   2006020467

1 2 3 4 5 6 7 8 9 10 R 17 16 15 14 13 12 11 10 09 08

As Americans set out from their homes to vote in the 2000 presidential election, some **polls** gave Democratic vice president Al Gore a narrow lead. Others put Republican Texas governor George W. Bush ahead by a slim margin. Still, no one could have expected that the morning after Election Day would arrive with no clear winner. It all came down to the state of Florida. Whoever won the Sunshine State would be the next president. But with Bush ahead by a very small amount, Gore called for a recount.

For weeks, the two sides filed lawsuits in Florida and federal courts attempting to make sure that the votes were recounted in a way that would favor their candidate. The case reached the United States Supreme Court twice. On December 4, in *Bush v. Palm Beach County*, the Court ordered the Florida Supreme Court to rethink its ruling allowing the recount to continue. The Florida Supreme Court ignored the U.S. Supreme Court and allowed recounting to go on. This resulted in the case being brought back to the U.S. Supreme Court as *Bush v. Gore*. Oral arguments were held on December 11, with lawyers for each side traveling to Washington, D.C., to speak before the nine justices.

Late the next evening, the justices announced their decision. A 5-to-4 majority said that the recount process being used in Florida, which differed from county to county, was **unconstitutional**. This decision meant the recount had to stop. As a result, George W. Bush, who had already been certified as the winner of Florida's **electoral votes**, won the election.

THE CONSTITUTIONAL CONVENTION

When American patriots formally adopted the Declaration of Independence on July 4, 1776, there was still much work to be done to set up the new nation. First, they had to finish the war against Britain, then create a government. But most Americans were so tired of living under a powerful king, they were afraid a powerful government could be just as bad.

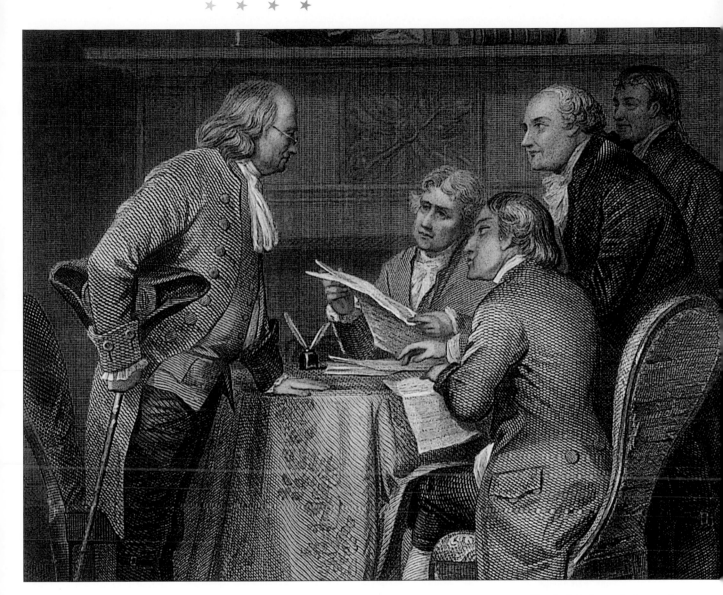

So in 1781, the leaders of the young United States created the Articles of Confederation, a sort of pre-Constitu-
tion, that gave almost no power to the central government.
In fact, it defined the country as no more than "a firm
league of friendship" among the thirteen states. There was
a Congress, but it couldn't make the states pay taxes or

A copy of the Bill of Rights

THE BILL OF RIGHTS

Before some states agreed to ratify, or accept, the new Constitution, they insisted that a statement of basic rights be included. On December 15, 1791, the first ten amendments, or changes, were added to the Constitution. They became known as the Bill of Rights. They guarantee Americans individual freedoms—from freedom of speech and religion to the right to keep and bear arms.

raise an army. There were no courts to enforce laws. There wasn't even a president. Each state could consider itself an independent nation and make just about any laws it wanted. Sometimes those laws were unfair. Some states were even denying people the very rights they had fought the Revolution for—and the central government had no power to stop it.

During the summer of 1787, U.S. leaders met in Philadelphia to write a Constitution. After a long, hot summer of debate, they devised a new government with three branches. The executive branch would be made up of a president, who would serve a four-year term. The legislative branch would consist of the Congress, which would be made up of the House of Representatives and the Senate. The judicial branch would be made up of courts, which would administer the nation's laws.

The **delegates** to the Constitutional Convention made sure that their new government had what are known as checks and balances. For every power they gave to one branch of government, they gave another branch a way to control that power. No president or Congress could do something without the support of another branch of government. For example, the president was given the right to **veto** a law

The U.S. Constitution went into effect on March 4, 1789.

John Jay was a member of Congress and the governor of New York before becoming the first chief justice.

that has been passed by Congress. But Congress can then override that veto with a vote by two-thirds of its members. Another example occurs if the president wants to go to war. Congress needs to issue a formal declaration of war. Meanwhile, the courts enforce the nation's laws.

Though the Constitution called for the establishment of a Supreme Court, it didn't specify its exact duties, saying only, "The judicial Power of the United States, shall be vested in one supreme Court, and in such inferior Courts as the Congress may from time to time ordain and establish." Indeed, the Constitution left it to Congress to figure out how the American court system should work. The U.S. Senate rose to the challenge: the first bill it introduced was the Judiciary Act of 1789, a bill that divided the country into thirteen judicial districts. These districts were further organized into the Eastern, Middle, and Southern circuits. The law stated that the Supreme Court should consist of a chief justice and five associate justices.

A SLOW START

In the country's early years, the judiciary was the weakest branch of government. Indeed, most of the appointed justices didn't take the job seriously. On the day of the Court's first session, only three of the six justices bothered to show up. John Jay, the first chief justice of the Supreme Court, spent most of his term traveling overseas. Another justice, John Rutledge, served for two years but resigned after becoming bored by the lack of activity.

Though their initial meeting was in 1790, the new justices did not hear their first case until 1792. A year later, their first truly important ruling was quickly overturned. In 1777, the state of Georgia bought some military equipment from Alexander Chisholm of South Carolina, but did not pay for it. The issue eventually went to the courts. In *Chisholm v. Georgia*, the Supreme Court ruled in favor of Chisholm. But the lawmakers in Congress believed that the Court had made the wrong decision. As a result, on March 4, 1794, Congress ratified the Eleventh Amendment to the Constitution, which limited the ability of federal, or U.S. government, courts to hear cases brought against a state by the citizens of another state.

★ ★ ★ ★

Given the Court's limits at the start, it seemed that the Court was destined to remain the weakest branch of government. But in fact, the Court had hidden advantages that gave it great power. Unlike senators and representatives, justices did not have to run for office every few years. Appointed to a life term, a Supreme Court justice could speak his mind without fear of being voted off the Court. Equally important was the way the Supreme Court is described in the Constitution. Section 2, Article III, says, "The judicial Power shall extend to all Cases, in Law and Equity, arising under this Constitution." Many early leaders believed that the Court existed for the sole purpose of resolving disputes between the states and the other two branches of government. But the language in the Constitution was vague enough that the Court's true powers were open to interpretation.

MARBURY V. MADISON

Today, most Americans belong to the Republican Party or the Democratic Party. Likewise, the turn of the nineteenth century was also dominated by two political parties. The Federalists were led by George Washington and Alexander Hamilton and believed in a strong central government. The Democratic-Republicans were led by Thomas Jefferson and believed that most government power should be retained by the individual states.

Today, presidents try to appoint judges who share their political outlook. The same was true in the early days of the United States. In 1800, John Adams, the nation's second president and a staunch Federalist, was defeated for reelection by Thomas Jefferson. In the last weeks of his presidency, Adams and the Federalist Congress created dozens of new judgeships and appointed forty-two Federalist judges to fill them. The most important appointment was John Marshall, Adams's secretary of state, as chief justice of the Supreme Court—a position he held until 1835.

It didn't take Marshall long to assert new and dramatic power for the Supreme Court. In 1803, the Court agreed to review a case called *Marbury v. Madison*, which arose out of Adams's rush to appoint Federalist judges in the final days of his presidency. A man named William Marbury was appointed to a position on a lower court. But when Thomas Jefferson took office, his secretary of state, James Madison (who later became the country's fourth president), refused to grant Marbury his position. Marbury appealed the case to the Supreme Court.

John Adams

AT VALLEY FORGE

As a young man, John Marshall served as a soldier in the Revolutionary War, spending the long, cold winter of 1777 at Valley Forge, Pennsylvania. While the individual states were unable to send blankets and food, Marshall watched fellow soldiers starve and die of various illnesses. It was then that he learned the importance of a strong central government, which could have sent the needed supplies.

U.S. Supreme Court chief justice John Marshall

Thomas Jefferson

Upon reviewing the case, Marshall found himself in a tricky situation. With the Supreme Court so poorly regarded by the American public, if Marshall ruled in favor of Marbury, he suspected that President Jefferson would ignore the ruling. This would weaken the Court. On the other hand, if Marshall ruled against Marbury, the Supreme Court would appear to be a tool of the Jefferson administration.

Marshall's solution was brilliant. After declaring that Marbury was entitled to his position, Marshall stated that

THOMAS JEFFERSON

A Democratic-Republican, Thomas Jefferson hated the way Chief Justice John Marshall asserted the federal government's power over the states. He called Marshall a "twistifier of the law."

★ ★ ★ ★

Marbury's appeal wasn't proper for the Supreme Court to consider. His reasoning was based on the Judiciary Act of 1789, the law that gave the Supreme Court the right to make decisions in cases such as this one. Marshall said that Congress had overstepped its bounds. Claiming that certain sections of the Judiciary Act were unconstitutional, he said that the Court could not instate Marbury to his post.

Justice Samuel Chase was so unpopular that some members of Congress named their vicious dogs after him.

In so doing, Marshall introduced the country to the concept of judicial review, or the right of the Court to review the laws passed by Congress and to call them unconstitutional. As Marshall wrote in his opinion, "A law [incompatible] to the constitution is void." In one bold stroke, Marshall made it clear that the Supreme Court had the enormous power to strike down federal laws and shape the workings of the government.

THE *DRED SCOTT* DECISION

For the first twenty-four years that John Marshall was chief justice, Presidents Jefferson, James Madison, and James Monroe—all Democratic-Republicans—appointed justices who supported their views on the issues of the day. But to their dismay, Marshall was such a clear thinker and powerful advocate of his opinions that he usually got the new justices to agree with him. During his tenure, Marshall's decisions came down again and again on the side of the federal government over the rights of the states. Marshall was so influential that John Adams said, "My gift of John Marshall to the people of the United States was the proudest act of my life."

The Supreme Court's next chief justice is not remembered as fondly. Roger Taney was born in 1777 in Maryland, a slave state. When Taney was confirmed as President Andrew Jackson's choice to replace Marshall as chief justice, many Federalists worried that he would destroy the Court. However, Justice Taney surprised his critics by ruling fairly and upholding many opinions of the Marshall Court.

Despite a distinguished career, Justice Taney, who served on the Court from 1836 to 1864, is remembered today for one disastrous opinion. By the 1850s, the issue of slavery was fast bringing the country to the brink of war. Many Southerners believed that slavery should be legal. Many Northerners

THE IMPEACHED JUSTICE

With John Marshall as the chief justice, the Democratic-Republicans became increasingly unhappy with the Supreme Court's rulings. Congress had especially bad feelings for Justice Samuel Chase. In 1804, Congress tried to change the makeup of the Court through impeachment and charged Justice Chase with committing crimes. But it became clear he was not guilty of any wrongdoing, and in March 1805, he was cleared of all charges. This was an important ruling. It ensured John Marshall and all the justices that they could issue opinions without fear of being removed from the Court.

Chief Justice Roger Taney had a long, distinguished career on the Court, but he is remembered only for his disastrous ruling, the *Dred Scott* decision.

Many southern slaves were bought and sold in markets such as this one.

believed the slaves should be free. At the heart of the slavery issue were disagreements about government power. In general, Northerners accepted the idea of a strong federal government and Southerners believed strongly in states' rights.

On March 4, 1857, James Buchanan took the oath of office as the United States' fifteenth president. In his inaugural address, Buchanan expressed hope that the courts would find a solution to the country's slavery problem. Two days later, Justice Taney ruled on *Scott v. Sandford*. It was one of the worst decisions in the history of the Court.

The facts of the case were fairly straightforward. Dr. John Emerson was a U.S. Army surgeon who spent several years at a number of different posts, some of which were located in

TANEY'S DECISION

In the *Dred Scott* decision, Taney discussed the history of blacks in America: "They had for more than a century before been regarded as beings of an inferior order; and altogether unfit to associate with the white race . . . and so far inferior that they had no rights. . . ."

northern Free States. During this time, Emerson was accompanied by a slave named Dred Scott. When Emerson died in 1846, Scott sued for his freedom, arguing that his time spent living in Free States made him a free man. After many years, the case reached the U.S. Supreme Court.

Justice Taney's opinion made three main points. First, Taney wrote, blacks were not considered U.S. citizens. Therefore, Scott was not allowed to sue in federal court. Though the Court could have thrown out the case, Taney went further. He held that a slave was private property and would therefore always remain a slave, even if he or she accompanied an owner to Free States. Finally, the Court held that a series of compromises between the North and the South aimed at limiting slave territory in the country were unconstitutional.

Though Taney had hoped to resolve ongoing disputes over the issue of slavery, his opinion only made things worse. While many Southerners were pleased, Northern abolitionists were furious. Within the next four years, the country was at war. After the *Dred Scott* decision, the American public largely forgot about Taney's early work on the Court. One observer said, "There was no sadder figure to be seen in Washington during the years of the Civil War [than Justice Taney]."

"SEPARATE BUT EQUAL"

In 1863, during the Civil War, President Abraham Lincoln signed the Emancipation Proclamation, declaring the freedom of all slaves in Confederate territory not already under

* * * *

Union control. Its immediate effect was to free only some runaway slaves. Two years later, the North won the war and Congress passed a series of amendments to the Constitution to protect the rights of former slaves. The Civil Rights Act of 1873 guaranteed all Americans full and equal use of theaters, inns, and "other places of public amusement . . . regardless of any previous condition of servitude."

Many of the Supreme Court's important cases during the years following the Civil War concerned the new civil rights that Congress had granted to black Americans. The Court's decisions resulted in many of those rights being taken away. In 1883, a series of civil rights cases reached the Court, filed against public theaters in New York City and San Francisco, a restaurant in Topeka, Kansas, a hotel in Jefferson City, Missouri, and a railroad in Tennessee— all of which were places that refused to serve blacks. Eight of nine Supreme Court justices rejected the lawsuits, arguing that the Civil Rights Act of 1873 was unconstitutional.

SIZE OF THE COURT

In the country's early years, the number of justices on the Supreme Court changed. At first, the Court consisted of six justices. In 1807, Congress increased the number to seven, due to population growth in the West. In 1837, the Court's size grew to nine and went up to ten during the Civil War. The number of justices was reduced to eight in 1866. Three years later, the number of justices on the Court was finally set at nine, where it has remained ever since.

There was one judge who disagreed. As a former slaveholder who had agreed with the *Dred Scott* decision, Justice John Harlan was an unlikely champion for equal rights. Yet during his thirty-four years on the Court, Harlan wrote 316 **dissenting** opinions, many in the defense of civil rights. A justice who is on the losing side of a decision can write an opinion called a dissent stating why he or she voted against the majority. In 1883, Harlan wrote, "Our Constitution is color blind and neither knows nor tolerates classes among its citizens." By that time, he regretted his previous support for the *Dred Scott* decision.

Harlan's best-known dissent came after another of the Supreme Court's most famous decisions, in *Plessy v. Ferguson*, in 1896. The case involved Homer Plessy, a man who was seven-eighths white and one-eighth black, and a Louisiana law that separated railroad cars by race. When Plessy tried to sit in the train car reserved for whites only, he was arrested. Plessy fought all the way to the Supreme Court. An 8-to-1 majority declared that "enforced separation of the two races does not mean unequal." The Court went on to state that "separate but equal" facilities were legal. Of course, the problem was that facilities in the South were already separate, but they were

John Harlan

A MIXED RECORD

During the post–Civil War years, the Court often ruled in favor of big businesses at the expense of workers. For example, the Court ruled that the few companies that controlled 98 percent of the sugar business were not **monopolies**. The Court also imprisoned striking workers for "restraining trade."

The Supreme Court often favored businesses, such as the sugar company that owned this warehouse in Colorado, over workers.

Stores such as this one marked "White Only" were a common sight in many states until the mid-1950s.

not equal. As a result, this ruling gave states permission to continue to do what they were already doing: **segregating** public schools, railroad cars, restaurants, and theaters. It would take more than fifty years for the Court's decision to be reversed.

JUDGE HARLAN DISSENTS

In *Plessy v. Ferguson*, Judge Harlan was the lone dissenter.

He wrote: "We boast of the freedom enjoyed by our people above all other peoples. But it is difficult to [make that boast consistent] with a state of the law which, practically, puts the brand of [slavery] . . . upon a large class of our fellow-citizens, our equals before the law."

Railroad cars, such as this dining car, were segregated. The only black Americans on board whites-only cars were servers.

★ ★ ★ ★

THE NEW DEAL

The first twenty years of the twentieth century were marked by what historians have called the Progressive Era. This was a time when Presidents Theodore Roosevelt (1901–1909) and Woodrow Wilson (1913–1921) signed a series of laws designed to protect the rights of workers and to limit the power of big businesses. Accordingly, many cases ruled on by the Supreme Court concerned these issues. Often, the Court proved unwilling to allow Congress to write laws that tried to fix various social problems.

In *Lochner v. New York* (1905), the Court said that the State of New York did not have the right to limit the working hours of bakers to ten a day. In 1918, Congress tried to stop employers from taking advantage of children by passing a law that forbade interstate shipment of any products made with child labor. The Court ruled the law unconstitutional. In 1923, the Court struck down a law that established a minimum wage for workingwomen.

On October 29, 1929, the **stock market** crashed. Overnight, many Americans lost their jobs and all their money.

Theodore Roosevelt

In the early 1900s, child laborers, such as this boy making baskets in an Indiana factory, were common.

The country was plunged into the Great Depression, one of the worst economic crises in history. In 1932, the country elected Franklin D. Roosevelt president. Roosevelt passed a series of laws aimed at repairing the nation's economy. The programs and policies he created were called the New Deal.

While the American public applauded Roosevelt's efforts, the Supreme Court had other ideas. One of Roosevelt's programs was the National Recovery Administration (NRA),

This famous photograph, called "Migrant Mother," shows Florence Thompson and her children. The Great Depression left many American families poor and hungry. Roosevelt's New Deal policies were created to help these families.

One of the most influential justices on the Court during the first part of the twentieth century was Oliver Wendell Holmes. During a time when the Court was quick to call congressional laws unconstitutional, Holmes warned his fellow justices that they should not strike down laws just because they differed from their own beliefs and opinions.

an organization that attempted to stabilize the economy by introducing codes, or rules, to regulate wages and working conditions. The NRA codes were written by trade associations and industry members. In May 1935, the Court ruled unanimously in *Schechter Poultry Corp. v. United States* that the NRA was unconstitutional because it gave lawmaking power to an outside group. In the end, the Court struck down eleven New Deal programs.

Roosevelt was furious. He believed the members of the Court were old and out of touch with the troubled times of the depression. Emboldened by his reelection landslide in 1936, Roosevelt revived a proposal the following year that would allow the president to appoint an additional justice for each member over the age of seventy. The American public saw Roosevelt's "court-packing" scheme as a power grab. The Senate refused to pass the law, and Roosevelt was forced to withdraw his proposal.

Eventually, however, Roosevelt got the Court he wanted. Some of the elderly justices died. Others quit, lured by a newly passed law that guaranteed full pay to any retiring justice over age seventy. This gave Roosevelt the opportunity to nominate the judges he knew would favor his programs. After the Senate approved their nominations and they were sworn in to serve on the Court, Roosevelt's New Deal legislation received its stamp of approval.

THE WARREN COURT

Although the makeup of the Supreme Court had changed, the "separate but equal" position established in *Plessy v. Ferguson* had not been reconsidered. Dissents from Justice Hugo Black in civil rights cases that came before the Court challenged the justices to guarantee basic rights to all Americans. Black was a former member of the Ku Klux Klan (KKK) who eventually fought for the rights of black

28

Thurgood Marshall (center) was a black lawyer from Baltimore, Maryland, who argued the case of *Brown v. Board of Education of Topeka* before the Supreme Court. In 1967, Marshall became the first black justice to serve on the Court.

* * * *

Americans and the poor. Still, it wasn't until the 1950s that the Court finally took action.

Leading the Court was Chief Justice Earl Warren, a former governor of California. When placed on the Court by President Dwight D. Eisenhower, Warren was thought to be a moderate, which means he did not have strong opinions on one side or the other of an issue. But Warren proved himself to be **liberal**, prompting Eisenhower to call placing him on the Court "the biggest . . . mistake I ever made."

Perhaps Warren's most important decision was one of his first. In the early 1950s, Oliver Brown, a black minister, tried to enroll his daughter Linda in a whites-only elementary school in Topeka, Kansas. In 1954, the case called *Brown v. Board of Education of Topeka* reached the Supreme Court. Earl Warren proceeded carefully. With an issue that provoked strong feelings among Americans, he wanted the Court's decision to be unanimous, or agreed on by everyone. He convinced his fellow justices that the time had come to put an end to segregation.

On May 17, 1954, Warren read his ruling: "We conclude that in the field of public education the doctrine of 'separate but equal' has no place. Separate educational facili-

Earl Warren

L. B. Sullivan (second from left) sued the *New York Times*.

ties are . . . unequal." More than fifty years after *Plessy v. Ferguson*, the Court ruled that American public schools must be desegregated.

Throughout the 1960s, the Warren Court handed down a series of sometimes **controversial** opinions. In *Engle v. Vitale* (1962), the Court ruled that it was unconstitutional for state officials to compose an official school prayer and require its recitation in public schools. In 1964, the Court gave a boost to supporters of freedom of the press when it ruled in *New York Times Company v. Sullivan* that for a person to sue a newspaper for **libel**, he

EARL WARREN

As chief justice from 1953 to 1969, Earl Warren was known to stray from legal arguments to ask attorneys commonsense questions. Since then, members of the Court have done the same.

Pro-choice and pro-life supporters demonstrating outside the U.S. Supreme Court

or she must be able to prove that the paper was knowingly lying. In *Griswold v. Connecticut* (1965), the Court asserted that the Constitution protected a right to privacy. This decision would have long-term implications eight years later, when the Court upheld women's right to **abortion**.

ROE V. WADE

Today, the right of a woman to end a pregnancy through a medical procedure called an abortion is one of the most controversial issues in the country. Much of the uproar has to do with the landmark Supreme Court decision issued on January 22, 1973, called *Roe v. Wade*. The Court decided by a 7-to-2 margin that a woman has a constitutional right to get an abortion during the first three months of a pregnancy. This decision was based in the Court's interpretation of several amendments of the Constitution as guaranteeing a fundamental right to privacy. The Court's ruling declared that most laws restricting or prohibiting abortion were in violation of this right.

The *Roe v. Wade* decision is still hotly debated. Many feel that laws concerning abortion should be decided at the state level. Because the right to privacy is not stated directly in the Constitution, opponents of the decision feel that the Court strayed too far from the actual text in their interpretation. Supporters of the *Roe v. Wade* ruling believe the rights provided by the decision are necessary to preserve women's equality and personal freedom.

MIRANDA V. ARIZONA

In 1966, in *Miranda v. Arizona*, the Court overturned the conviction of Ernesto Miranda, a man accused of raping and kidnapping a woman, because the police had forced him to **incriminate** himself. The Warren Court asserted that during arrest, all criminal defendants must be read what is now called the Miranda warning.

Ernesto Miranda

John Paul Stevens is the longest-serving member of the Court. He was sworn in as a justice in 1975.

✷ ✷ ✷ ✦

Though some Americans welcomed the decision as upholding the basic rights of every American, others were outraged. To them, the Warren Court was more concerned with the rights of criminals than with the rights of victims.

Today, many Americans have accepted most of the rulings issued by the Warren Court. But some decisions—especially those concerning school prayer, abortion, and the *Miranda* warning—remain controversial.

MIRANDA WARNING

The *Miranda* ruling states that anyone who is arrested "must be warned prior to any questioning that he has the right to remain silent, that anything he says can be used against him in a court of law, that he has the right to the presence of an attorney, and that if he cannot afford an attorney one will be appointed for him prior to any questioning if he so desires."

THE SUPREME COURT TODAY

During the late twentieth and early twenty-first centuries, the Supreme Court continued to struggle with important

President Bill Clinton applauds Judge Ruth Bader Ginsburg after he announces her nomination as the second woman to serve on the Court.

William H. Rehnquist served as chief justice of the Supreme Court from 1986 until his death in 2005.

constitutional questions. Though President Bill Clinton, a Democrat, nominated two liberal justices when he was in office, Republican presidents Ronald Reagan, George H. W. Bush, and George W. Bush, have nominated liberal and **conservative** justices. As a result, today's Court is sometimes split on important rulings.

37

President George W. Bush announces the nomination of John G. Roberts as chief justice of the Supreme Court to replace William Rehnquist. Roberts was confirmed by the Senate on September 29, 2005.

* * * *

A new term of the Supreme Court begins each year on the first Monday in October. Arguments before the nine justices usually last only one hour. Later, when discussing a case, the nine justices sit around a table in order of seniority. The newest justice sits near the door so he or she can respond in case someone knocks.

The Court says that it receives "a current total of more than 7,000 cases on the docket per Term." The Court says "Formal written opinions are delivered in 80–90 cases. Approximately 50–60 additional cases are disposed of without granting plenary review." Despite differences

The U.S. Supreme Court building in Washington, D.C.

In early 2006, the justices
of the U.S. Supreme Court
gathered for this photo.

Back row, from left: Justice
Stephen Breyer, Justice
Clarence Thomas, Justice
Ruth Bader Ginsburg,
Justice Samuel Alito

Front row, from left: Justice
Anthony Kennedy, Justice
John Paul Stevens, Chief
Justice John Roberts, Jus-
tice Antonin Scalia, Justice
David Souter

in the Court between conservatives and liberals, many of those opinions are unanimous—indeed, the members of the Supreme Court tend to agree with each other more often than not. Still, some opinions are hard to predict. As Maureen Mahoney, a law clerk to Chief Justice William Rehnquist, said, "It is often the surprising rulings that have the broadest impact on Americans."

While some Americans in 1954 were surprised by the ruling in *Brown v. Board of Education of Topeka*, today most everyone agrees that the decision changed American

public education for the better. Similarly, it is now commonly believed that Justice Taney's *Dred Scott* decision was a disaster that helped speed the country into Civil War. Other decisions remain controversial.

Even so, most Americans agree that they are fortunate to live in a country where the law is respected and obeyed. For more than two hundred years, the Supreme Court has interpreted those laws, helping to make the United States the most successful democracy in the world.

Glossary

abortion—the ending of a pregnancy by a medical procedure

amendments—changes that are made to a law or a legal document

conservative—traditional; usually favoring individual freedom more than government control

controversial—causing a lot of argument

delegates—people who represent other people at a meeting

dissenting—disagreeing with an established opinion or idea

electoral votes—votes cast by state officials called electors usually based on the results of that state's popular vote (the vote of the people); whoever wins a majority of electoral votes becomes president of the United States

impeachment—the process of bringing formal charges against a public official who may have committed a crime or done something wrong while in office

incriminate—to show that someone is guilty of a crime or another wrong action

libel—a written statement that is unjust or untrue

liberal—nontraditional; usually favoring government control more than individual freedom

monopolies—companies that have complete control over a service or the supply of a product

polls—surveys of people's opinions or beliefs

segregating—dividing, particularly based on race, class, gender, or ethnicity

stock market—the place where money is invested and traded

unconstitutional—not in keeping with the basic principles or laws set forth in the Constitution

veto—to stop a bill from becoming a law by refusing to approve it

Timeline: The Supreme

1789	1790	1803	1857	1896	1916	1937

MARCH 4
The U.S. Constitution goes into effect.

SEPTEMBER 24
Congress passes the Judiciary Act of 1789, which sets up the U.S. court system.

FEBRUARY 1
The Supreme Court meets for the first time.

FEBRUARY 24
In *Marbury v. Madison*, the Court claims the right to judge congressional laws unconstitutional.

MARCH 6
In *Scott v. Sandford*, the Court rules that a slave is always property.

MAY 18
In *Plessy v. Ferguson*, the Court rules segregation is legal.

Louis Brandeis becomes the first Jewish justice to serve on the Court.

Franklin D. Roosevelt tries unsuccessfully to pack the Court with additional justices.

Court

1954	**1967**	**1973**	**1981**	**2000**	**2005**	**2006**
MAY 17 Chief Justice Earl Warren delivers unanimous decision that leads to desegregating the nation's public schools.	Thurgood Marshall becomes the first African American to serve on the Court.	**JANUARY 22** In *Roe v. Wade*, the Court rules women may undergo abortion in the first three months of pregnancy.	Sandra Day O'Connor becomes the first woman to serve on the Court.	**DECEMBER 12** In *Bush v. Gore*, the Court rules the Florida recount is unconstitutional.	John Roberts becomes the Court's seventeenth chief justice.	Samuel Alito is sworn in as a justice. He replaces Sandra Day O'Connor.

45

To Find Out More

BOOKS

Giddens-White, Bryon. *The Supreme Court and the Judicial Branch.* Chicago: Heinemann, 2005.

January, Brendan. *The Supreme Court.* Danbury, Conn.: Franklin Watts, 2005.

Lewis, Lois. *America's Leaders: The Chief Justice.* San Diego: Blackbirch Press, 2002.

Smalley, Carol Parenzan. *The Judicial Branch.* Logan, Iowa: Perfection Learning, 2005.

ONLINE SITES

The Supreme Court of the United States
http://www.supremecourtus.gov

The Supreme Court Historical Society
http://www.supremecourthistory.org

Time for Kids, The Supreme Court
http://www.timeforkids.com/TFK/specials

Index

About the Author

Dan Elish is the author of numerous books for children, including *The Worldwide Dessert Contest* and *Born Too Short: The Confessions of an Eighth-Grade Basket Case*, which was picked as a 2003 Book for the Teen Age by the New York Public Library. He lives in New York City with his wife and two children.